THINK THESE THINGS

99 Meditative Messages To Make Your Day

Copyright © 2016 Quentin McCain & E. Marie Hall

ThinkonTheseThingsBook.com

ISBN-13: 978-0692709658 (Abundant Press)
ISBN-10: 0692709657

Printed in the United States of America

Abundant Press
Publish - Promote - Profit - Position - Platform
AbundantPress.com

Printed by:

Register this Book

ThinkonTheseThingsBook.com

To Access Additional Bonuses

DEDICATIONS

This book is dedicated to Elsie and Elijah Howard who took me in at the age of two. You showed me love and gave me lifelong tools. You taught me courage, determination and, most importantly, faith. I will forever think on these things. I am who I am because of you.

- E. Marie Hall

This book is also dedicated to the smartest girl I know, my daughter, Alyssa McCain. When I look into your eyes it gives me hope and keeps me strong. In every smile you give me, I see faith. You can do anything you put your mind to, baby girl. Always THINK on the positive aspect of every situation and the world will be your playground!

- Quentin McCain

CONTENTS

Foreword by Wyatt Earp
Introduction

FOREWORD

It is said, what we think about most, we become. Never have I seen a more practical and simple method for making this happen without great effort than in "Think On These Things." Over the years there have been many books written on the power of positive thinking. However, "Think On These Things" brings an updated perspective on how to be successful and how to allow and maintain happiness in our lives.

I have spent most of my life both professionally and athletically envisioning how to make my goals come to fruition. Through the years I achieved much success as a "Million Dollar Round Table Member" in the insurance business. I have competed in fifty triathlons, including two of the Hawaiian Iron Man events. I have been able to launch a successful acting career in retirement and have performed my one-man bio dramas in over one thousand fifty performances. All of this was made possible due to finding a way to think of myself as being successful in all of these endeavors.

E. Marie Hall and her son Quentin McCain have created a book full of methods for personal success that actually work in today's world. "Think On These Things" is a page-turner that will help you chart your course to a more productive and enriching life.

Wyatt Earp *www.wyattearp.biz*

INTRODUCTION

It began as just a thought, like all things. We had been on a personal development journey which brought us to a moment of truth. Reading something positive when you awake can set the tone for your entire day. Not only is this beneficial in the morning, but the last thoughts before going to sleep also have an influence.

So, we began to write with the only goal being to make an impact, to enrich the lives of others. Little did we know…that "thought", would take on a totally different form from what we envisioned.

Our hope is that you read and meditate on these messages daily. You now hold in your hand, the project that began with

just a "thought." THINK ON THESE THINGS.

DAY 1
THE PROCESS OF PROGRESS

One thing we've discovered—
if you never start, it is certain

You will never finish.

Progress is progress, regardless of the
time frame. But, it's your life—you set
the pace!

Here is the secret--get started!

What steps will you take today that
will move you forward?

DAY 1

THE PROCESS OF PROGRESS

What steps will you take today that will move you forward?

THOUGHTS/ACTION STEPS

DAY 2

THE GOLDEN OPPORTUNITY

Pick up the mirror and take a long, hard look at Mr/Ms Opportunity.

Everything you need, you already have. Give yourself what you've been yearning for. Wait no longer!

Get up and make it happen—take advantage of this opportunity called life!

Can you see any opportunities in a current challenge?

DAY 2

THE GOLDEN OPPORTUNITY

Can you see any opportunities in a current challenge?

THOUGHTS/ACTION STEPS

_____

_____

_____

_____

_____

_____

_____

_____

_____

_____

_____

_____

_____

_____

_____

_____

_____

DAY 3

<u>BIG BREAK</u>

Believe it--and it will come.

Focus on it-- and it will come.

Work at it-- and it will come-- at the right time in the right way.

Rest assured, there will come a day.

Make each move intentional, because it is all about how you **PLAY** the game of life.

What would a big break look like to you?

DAY 3

<u>BIG BREAK</u>

What would a big break look like to you?

THOUGHTS/ACTION STEPS

DAY 4
<u>NO BRAINER</u>

If you use your brain at all, you'll have some results; but if you truly use it properly you will generate incredible results!

You will not only transform your life, but the lives of others.

It's a no-brainer really.

DAY 4

NO BRAINER

THOUGHTS/ACTION STEPS

DAY 5
LET THE MUSIC PLAY

You may think the tune of your life has fallen off key, but the truth is the instrument is just a little dusty.

The life you have imagined is still ahead of you and it's all in your hands.

Knock the dirt off and stroke those strings so the world can hear your beautiful song!

List three things that could reignite Your sparks.

DAY 5

LET THE MUSIC PLAY

List three things that could reignite your sparks.

THOUGHTS/ACTION STEPS

DAY 6

TAP THE SOURCE

You have not even begun to tap into your power and potential.

Wouldn't you like to know just how far you can go—just how much you can achieve?

Why not put it to the test?

Find out what you're really made of.

Not only might you surprise others; but yourself as well.

Go ahead--take the challenge!

Think of a time when you achieved the "impossible".

DAY 6
TAP THE SOURCE

Think of a time when you achieved the "impossible".

THOUGHTS/ACTION STEPS

_____

_____

_____

_____

_____

_____

_____

_____

_____

_____

_____

_____

_____

_____

DAY 7

WHERE ARE YOU HEADED?

Where you are right now has absolutely no bearing on where you can end up.

Your destiny is determined by your level of commitment not your starting point.

YOU decide what you will do and where you will go.

The decision is yours--and only yours.

Make it up in your mind to start by either accepting or changing your circumstances.

NO MORE EXCUSES!

Choose an excuse to replace with a solution.

DAY 7

WHERE ARE YOU HEADED?

Choose an excuse to replace with a solution.

THOUGHTS/ACTION STEPS

DAY 8

WAIT NO MORE

Don't wait for the leader—be the leader!

Be the change, be the solution, be the person to make it happen.

Do it like it has never been done before—one person at a time; one small victory at a time; one success at a time!

And remember, wait broke the wagon down.

What is something you've been waiting to do? When will you do it?

DAY 8

<u>WAIT NO MORE</u>

What is something you've been waiting to do?

When will you do it?

THOUGHTS/ACTION STEPS

_____

_____

_____

_____

_____

_____

_____

_____

_____

_____

_____

_____

_____

_____

_____

DAY 9

<u>GET TO STEPPIN'</u>

It is virtually impossible to lose while taking steps.

With every step taken, you distance yourself! With every goal reached you minimize the gap between you and the dream.

Winners don't stop with the first step— the greater the separation the bigger the win.

But you've got to...TAKE THAT STEP!

What will step one be?

DAY 9

GET TO STEPPIN'

What will step one be?

THOUGHTS/ACTION STEPS

DAY 10

BOTTOMS UP

In most cases it is not a matter of whether or not you will hit the bottom.

Chances are you will. In fact, you may feel as if you're there now.

But, assure yourself that remaining at the bottom is not an option.

The pressure that brought you down will give you the momentum to bounce back up.

DAY 10

<u>BOTTOMS UP</u>

THOUGHTS/ACTION STEPS

DAY 11

GIVE MORE—RECEIVE MORE

Everyone has the ability to help someone. But, the more you have—the more you have to give.

In fact, the more you are given, the more you are **REQUIRED** to give.

It's as simple as that.

List 5 ways you can give back.

DAY 11

<u>GIVE MORE—RECEIVE MORE</u>

List 5 ways you can give back.

THOUGHTS/ACTION STEPS

_____

_____

_____

_____

_____

_____

_____

_____

_____

_____

_____

_____

_____

_____

_____

_____

DAY 12

ARE YOU ALIVE?

Ok, let's state the obvious—you are alive, or at least have a pulse!

But, as long as the heart beats, we should be yearning to learn; burning to earn; accomplishing all upon which we set our sights.

It is an ongoing process; a lifelong journey.

Pack a lunch!

When was the last time you did something for the first time?

DAY 12

ARE YOU ALIVE?

When was the last time you did something for the first time?

THOUGHTS/ACTION STEPS

_____

_____

_____

_____

_____

_____

_____

_____

_____

_____

_____

_____

_____

_____

DAY 13

<u>GETTING TO KNOW YOU</u>

Your primary focus in life should be getting to know the primary person in your life—YOU.

Don't be afraid to allow yourself to be first.

For once you have truly accepted this concept, you will know that it matters not what anyone else says.

Have you made any new self-discoveries recently? What are they?

DAY 13

GETTING TO KNOW YOU

Have you made any new self-discoveries recently?

What are they?

THOUGHTS/ACTION STEPS

DAY 14

<u>WHO'S WITH ME?</u>

Evaluate your five closest friends today!

Surely, they would all ride in the limo; but how many would be waiting with you at the bus stop?

Does their loyalty lie with you or with your benefits?

When the going gets tough do they stick around or are they nowhere to be found?

Would you want to be YOUR friend?

DAY 14

WHO'S WITH ME?

Would you want to be YOUR friend?

THOUGHTS/ACTION STEPS

DAY 15

CHANGE

Be the change you talk about. Look life square in the eye.

Stand up to your challenges and face them head on.

Don't back down—don't be afraid to make adjustments—change is necessary.

And, who better to do it than you?

What are some things you can change immediately?

DAY 15

<u>CHANGE</u>

What are some things you can change immediately?

THOUGHTS/ACTION STEPS

DAY 16
<u>SUNRISE</u>

Focus on the morning—see the sunlight—know that things will get better.

You will laugh, you will smile--hard times are only here for a while.

See it, believe it, receive it!

Visualize and describe your ideal day.

What does that look like?

DAY 16

SUNRISE

Visualize and describe your ideal day.
What does that look like?

THOUGHTS/ACTION STEPS

DAY 17

FULLY ALIVE

The dictionary defines passion as a "strong and barely controllable emotion".

You need very little of it to play small. Coasting through life on automatic is easy—98% of the population does it.

But think--what would happen if you used that powerful emotion to live life to the fullest?

There is nothing you couldn't do; nowhere you couldn't go.

Why settle?

That's what dust does.

DAY 17

FULLY ALIVE

THOUGHTS/ACTION STEPS

_____

_____

_____

_____

_____

_____

_____

_____

_____

_____

_____

_____

_____

_____

DAY 18

UNSPOKEN

Is it helping or hurting?

In other words, it is better to remain silent than to speak negatively.

Oftentimes, no words are better than empty, unnecessary words.

Some things truly are better left unsaid.

The next time you disagree, sit with it rather than responding.

DAY 18

<u>UNSPOKEN</u>

The next time you disagree,
sit with it rather than responding.

THOUGHTS/ACTION STEPS

DAY 19

FAITH

Even the good book tells us it is the substance of things hoped for, the evidence of things not seen.

Just because you haven't gotten it, does not mean it's not there.

All things are possible if you would only believe.

What area of your life could use a little faith?

DAY 19

FAITH

What area of your life could use a little faith?

THOUGHTS/ACTION STEPS

DAY 20
WHAT WILL YOU CHOOSE?

Oftentimes two people brought up under the same conditions end up with totally different outcomes—one successful, one not.

Both had options but chose differently.

The path to your destiny is paved with the bricks of choice.

Pay close attention to your choices for the next week.

DAY 20

WHAT WILL YOU CHOOSE?

Pay close attention to your choices for the next week.

THOUGHTS/ACTION STEPS

DAY 21
YOUR CHOICE

So, what will it be?

Make the choice today!

But keep in mind the choice you make could affect the rest of your life.

Would you prefer a life of misery or a life of happiness—a life of abundance or a life of lack?

It is entirely up to you!

DAY 21

YOUR CHOICE

THOUGHTS/ACTION STEPS

_____

_____

_____

_____

_____

_____

_____

_____

_____

_____

_____

_____

_____

_____

_____

_____

_____

DAY 22

GARBAGE IN—GARBAGE OUT

The person sending out negative thoughts will surely bring back negative results.

If you let a stubbed toe, a flat tire or a traffic jam ruin the beginning of your day, expect it to remain and end the same way.

As you reap so shall you sow.
Plant positive seeds.

Nourish them, and they will grow.

What three positive seeds can you start planting?

DAY 22

GARBAGE IN—GARBAGE OUT

What three positive seeds can you start planting?

THOUGHTS/ACTION STEPS

DAY 23

<u>MIND OVER MATTER</u>

Anything that you have EVER imagined doing can be done.

If you can create it in your mind, it can be brought to fruition.

Rome was not built in a day—but it was built.

You need only focus and believe!

Recall a childhood dream.

Now let your imagination run wild!

DAY 23
MIND OVER MATTER

Recall a childhood dream. Now let
your imagination run wild!

THOUGHTS/ACTION STEPS

DAY 24

FLIGHT LESSON

That uncomfortable, uneasy feeling in the pit of your stomach—it's because you are creeping.

Your body, your mind, your soul wants to **SOAR**! Give it what it wants.

Get up off the ground, use your legs, try out your wings—soar baby, soar!

What would it take for you to soar into your next venture?

DAY 24

FLIGHT LESSON

What would it take for you to soar into
your next venture?

THOUGHTS/ACTION STEPS

DAY 25

PULSE CHECK

Are you breathing?

Are you reading this right now?

So, you are breathing AND reading this?! Well, that means you're alive—and where there is life there is hope.

THIS IS THE DAY TO GET MOVING!

The only thing it is too late for
IS EXCUSES.

List every excuse that comes to mind today. And, throw it away!

DAY 25

PULSE CHECK

List every excuse that comes to mind today.
And, throw it away!

THOUGHTS/ACTION STEPS

DAY 26

<u>INSIDE OUT</u>

You will never get all you want until you start being happy for what you have.

Happiness does not come because you are successful.

Success comes because you have learned to be happy.

It's from the inside out—not the outside in.

Think of ten things you are grateful for.

DAY 26

<u>INSIDE OUT</u>

Think of ten things you are grateful for.

THOUGHTS/ACTION STEPS

_____

_____

_____

_____

_____

_____

_____

_____

_____

_____

_____

_____

_____

_____

DAY 27

STILL SMALL VOICE

The inner voice is the real you and it can take you **ANYWHERE** you want to go.

It's begging to get out, screaming at you, whispering in your ear. It will follow you around everywhere!

IT MUST BE HEARD!
To ignore it could be fatal.

Think of a time when you followed your intuition.

DAY 27

STILL SMALL VOICE

Think of a time when you followed your intuition.

THOUGHTS/ACTION STEPS

DAY 28

WHAT'S YOUR PASSION SCORE?

Love life! Be the person you would want to be around.

Live full out—no holds barred!

After all, if you don't even love yourself, why on earth would you expect anybody else to?!

While a credit score might be attractive—a high passion score seals the deal.

Wouldn't you agree?

DAY 28

WHAT'S YOUR PASSION SCORE?

THOUGHTS/ACTION STEPS

DAY 29

<u>DARE TO BE GREAT!</u>

Do something—put forth the effort.

So what if it doesn't work out the first time! How will you know how far you can go or what you can do—unless you dare?

The world is waiting for you, take the risk.

Do it like it has **NEVER** been done before because after all it hasn't, by you.

What might make the difference that could change everything?

DAY 29

<u>DARE TO BE GREAT!</u>

What might make the difference that
could change everything?

THOUGHTS/ACTION STEPS

DAY 30

CAN YOU HEAR ME NOW?

Listening goes a long way, but actually hearing can save the day.

It is not just about listening to the words, it's about hearing the message, feeling the emotion, connecting with the speaker; and then perhaps, making use of the information.

Now, that is something to talk about.

What good news have you heard recently?

DAY 30

<u>CAN YOU HEAR ME NOW?</u>

What good news have you heard recently?

THOUGHTS/ACTION STEPS

_____

_____

_____

_____

_____

_____

_____

_____

_____

_____

_____

_____

_____

_____

DAY 31

METAMORPHOSIS

The end of one era oftentimes
represents the beginning of another.

It's all about transformation.

Like the caterpillar you too can
undergo drastic change.

Make your previous state
unrecognizable.

Spread your wings and fly!

What would be possible
if you underwent a total
transformation?

DAY 31

METAMORPHOSIS

What would be possible if you underwent a total transformation?

THOUGHTS/ACTION STEPS

_____

_____

_____

_____

_____

_____

_____

_____

_____

_____

_____

_____

_____

_____

DAY 32
<u>NO LIMITS</u>

Once we have figured out what we want and determined to give it our undivided attention; everything and everybody must step aside.

We cannot look to the left or to the right. It is full steam ahead! Eliminate all objections and obstacles; burn all bridges.

Allow no hindrances! The ultimate goal is abundance.

What recent steps have you taken toward your goal of an abundant life?

DAY 32

<u>NO LIMITS</u>

What recent steps have you taken toward your goal of
an abundant life?

THOUGHTS/ACTION STEPS

DAY 33

ASK

First things first—grant yourself permission to ask for what you want!

No one is going to ask for you.

And, nothing is too small or too great—it is never too early or too late.

But, it's not likely to just fall from the clouds.

Have some faith, believe in yourself and prepare to receive.

What will you ask for today?

DAY 33

ASK

What will you ask for today?

THOUGHTS/ACTION STEPS

DAY 34

DUST SETTLES—NOT YOU

Happiness is not synonymous with complacency.

We should be ever growing and ever learning—reaching for higher heights and deeper depths.

Never settle, there's always something more to aim for.

How have you stretched yourself this week?

DAY 34

<u>DUST SETTLES—NOT</u> <u>YOU</u>

How have you stretched yourself this week?

THOUGHTS/ACTION STEPS

DAY 35

TRUE COLORS

Which is more important character or reputation? Ideally, the two should match.

If we are indeed in alignment, there is little difference between what most people think of us and who we actually are.

Whatever your true character is, your reputation will eventually reveal.

Are you being real?

DAY 35

TRUE COLORS

Are you being real?

THOUGHTS/ACTION STEPS

DAY 36

GO FORWARD

It is not a loss until accepted as true.

Defeat is all about how it is viewed, allowing the circumstance to prevail over you.

Think of a set-back as an opportunity for a spring-back.

So, spring back and launch forward!

Repeat: spring back, launch forward.

DAY 36

GO FORWARD

Repeat: spring back, launch forward.

THOUGHTS/ACTION STEPS

DAY 37

MASTERPIECE

All that you need to succeed is within.

The sooner you come to this realization, the better your life will be.

Think of the acorn and how it becomes the magnificent oak tree.

Everything it requires is programmed in it--from the beginning.

DAY 37

<u>MASTERPIECE</u>

THOUGHTS/ACTION STEPS

DAY 38

<u>SAY MY NAME!</u>

First and foremost, we are all important!

One good tip which requires a small amount of effort is to remember names and use them.

Research says that people love the sound of their own name.

Make music to their ears.

Start today!

DAY 38

SAY MY NAME!

THOUGHTS/ACTION STEPS

DAY 39

DON'T WORRY, BE HAPPY

Don't chase it, accept it—make it up in your mind to have it.

Look around at all the many reasons to be grateful. Count your blessings!

Happiness is a state of mind.

The question to ask is, "What state is your mind in?" Believe you deserve happiness!

List three reasons you deserve to be happy.

DAY 39

<u>DON'T WORRY, BE</u> <u>HAPPY</u>

List three reasons you deserve to be happy.

THOUGHTS/ACTION STEPS

DAY 40
LASER FOCUS

Trying to master multiple things in multiple areas at once can prove to be disastrous.

It is very easy to get overwhelmed and in the end have nothing. Every great idea, pursued with faith and passion, will have its time.

Find that **ONE** thing and make it a force to be reckoned with!

Practice laser focus today.

DAY 40

LASER FOCUS

Practice laser focus today.

THOUGHTS/ACTION STEPS

DAY 41

IMMORTALITY

By all means do for yourself—but not ONLY for yourself.

Don't just make a mark, no half stepping, stomp your footprint in the soil of life.

The rewards will be reaped for generations to come. Leave a legacy!

Imagine you have lived the life of your dreams—now write your eulogy. Read aloud.

DAY 41
IMMORTALITY

Imagine you have lived the life of your dreams—
now write your eulogy. Read aloud.

THOUGHTS/ACTION STEPS

DAY 42
MOVE IT!

Get up, turn off the TV, this just in: The person responsible for your troubles—is you.

We sit too much anyway.

Shake it off, and move forward!

The first step is accepting responsibility, no matter what the condition.

Reduce distractions this week by cutting out at least one hour of TV, social media, etc. (You know what they are.)

DAY 42

MOVE IT!

Reduce distractions this week by cutting out at least one hour of TV, social media, etc. (You know what they are.)

THOUGHTS/ACTION STEPS

DAY 43
WELL READ

Obviously, you don't have to be reading this. Good choice!

Reading truly is fundamental. Continue to build on it.

Make it a habit to read something beneficial every single day.

That is the inspiration behind this book.

May it serve you well.

DAY 43

<u>WELL READ</u>

THOUGHTS/ACTION STEPS

DAY 44

PRO LIFE

Make learning a lifelong experience.

We will never know it all. If our hearts are still beating, there's more to learn.

Rest assured there is always room for growth. If you are not growing, you're dying.

Why not choose life?

Are you fully alive?

DAY 44

PRO LIFE

Are you fully alive?

THOUGHTS/ACTION STEPS

DAY 45

<u>LET GO!</u>

Leave the failures, faults and foes behind.

Forget who you thought you were and focus on who you desire to be.

Free the mind and the body will follow.

Become that passionate person of unlimited possibilities.

Let go and leap forward!

DAY 45

LET GO!

Let go and leap forward!

THOUGHTS/ACTION STEPS

DAY 46
<u>DO YOU</u>

We have to be ourselves no matter what people may say or think about it.

There will always be people backing you up and most likely even more against you; but we will just watch those people in the rearview mirror as we are driving our way up to success!

DAY 46

DO <u>YOU</u>

THOUGHTS/ACTION STEPS

_____
_____
_____
_____
_____
_____
_____
_____
_____
_____
_____
_____
_____
_____
_____
_____
_____

DAY 47

SEARCH AND DISCOVER

DON'T GIVE UP!

Look for new ideas, new relationships, new opportunities.

No's often mean not yet.

Keep searching, keep knocking, keep opening doors--persevere.

Success is near.

Make a list of possible opportunities.

DAY 47

SEARCH AND DISCOVER

Make a list of possible opportunities.

THOUGHTS/ACTION STEPS

DAY 48

<u>THE POWER WITHIN</u>

Go for it! Do not shrink, expand—give it your all.

Talents were given to use, to share, to multiply.

We all have those special qualities within us that we can give but can never be taken away.

Leave no stone unturned!

Which of your special qualities could you better utilize?

DAY 48

THE POWER WITHIN

Which of your special qualities could you better utilize?

THOUGHTS/ACTION STEPS

DAY 49
THE ULTIMATE CONQUEROR

Don't let your past draw out the blueprint for your future.

We have all had our ups and downs.

There is nothing new under the sun.

Someone has gone through what you have and prevailed.

Love conquers all.

Think of a time love prevailed.

DAY 49

THE ULTIMATE CONQUEROR

Think of a time love prevailed.

THOUGHTS/ACTION STEPS

_____
_____
_____
_____
_____
_____
_____
_____
_____
_____
_____
_____
_____
_____
_____
_____
_____

DAY 50

MAKE MY DAY

When you become too uncomfortable to remain where you are, you will change.

When you wake up and realize you simply cannot continue down the same path; you will change.

When the day-to-day grind literally drains your energy and you know for a fact, this couldn't possibly be it—then, and only then, will the growth process begin.

THIS is your lucky day!

DAY 50

MAKE MY DAY

THOUGHTS/ACTION STEPS

DAY 51

HOT WATER

Get out of the water!

If you can at least stick a toe out there is hope for the rest of your mind and body.

Do not give in to the currents, pull yourself up and out. So what things are a little soggy right now and you're in it up to your eyeballs.

I assure you, the sun will shine in your life again.

But, you will appreciate it a lot more once you have removed yourself from the water.

Think of an area of your life where you need resolution.

Can you start letting go today?

DAY 51

HOT WATER

Think of an area of your life where you need resolution.

Can you start letting go today?

THOUGHTS/ACTION STEPS

DAY 52
WAKE UP!

The means to be inspired is all around us, look for it, grasp it, and hold on to it.

Utilize that powerful mind you've been given.

Stop sleepwalking and take a ride to the wild side.

Start some fireworks—awaken the sleeping giant!

DAY 52

WAKE UP!

THOUGHTS/ACTION STEPS

DAY 53
KEEPING IT REAL

Action really does speak louder than words.

It doesn't matter what you say, if you're doing the opposite.

What you are doing and what you are saying should be in alignment.

Your actions must mirror your words and vice versa.

In other words--just keep it real!

Take a moment to think before you speak today.

DAY 53

KEEPING IT REAL

Take a moment to think before you speak today.

THOUGHTS/ACTION STEPS

_____
_____
_____
_____
_____
_____
_____
_____
_____
_____
_____
_____
_____
_____
_____
_____

DAY 54

THE GOLDEN RULE

Remember the golden rule?

Do unto others as you would have them do unto you.

Empower, inspire, and motivate others!

Help them develop, and in the process manifest their true selves.

See in them what they may not see in themselves.

In doing so, you enrich your own life as well.

Start by giving at least three authentic compliments today.

DAY 54

THE GOLDEN RULE

Start by giving at least three authentic compliments today.

THOUGHTS/ACTION STEPS

DAY 55

<u>DEFINITE PURPOSE</u>

How bad do you want it?

What are you willing to sacrifice for it?

Do you even know what "IT" is?

These are the questions we must ask in order to get the answers we must have.

Know what you want even if you haven't figured out how to get it yet.

Have a purpose that is definite.

Put your definite purpose in writing and read it out loud.

DAY 55

DEFINITE PURPOSE

Put your definite purpose in writing and read it out loud.

THOUGHTS/ACTION STEPS

DAY 56

UNINTERRUPTED

Just do it!

Do not concern yourself with what others say or whether or not it has been done before.

Nothing was done, before it was done the first time.

Don't let anyone interrupt you.

Stay focused and ignore the haters!

What will you do today?

DAY 56

UNINTERRUPTED

What will you do today?

THOUGHTS/ACTION STEPS

DAY 57

<u>GO FORWARD</u>

Make a move--at least give it a shot!
Inquire about it.

Very few people, if any, have success
just dropped in their laps.

Don't sit around waiting for it--make it
happen.

In the words of my late father, Elijah
Howard—GO FORWARD!!

DAY 57

GO FORWARD

THOUGHTS/ACTION STEPS

DAY 58
LEAVE A TRAIL

Make your own way--don't follow the "in-crowd".

Majority does not always rule though it may seem more appealing in the moment.

Sometimes we may feel as if we have no idea how to make a name for ourselves.

A life of gratitude, positivity and a little elbow grease can lead the way for others to follow!

DAY 58

LEAVE A TRAIL

THOUGHTS/ACTION STEPS

DAY 59
LIMITLESS BOUNDARIES

We have no limitations besides our own minds!!

We can do anything we truly want to do. It has been proven over and over again by people who have made disabilities into motivators and have made situations of poverty and heartache do a complete 180!

To achieve success we must ignore what people say we "can't" do and think on the things we can!

What can you do to move outside your comfort zone?

DAY 59
LIMITLESS BOUNDARIES

What can you do to move outside your comfort zone?

THOUGHTS/ACTION STEPS

_____
_____
_____
_____
_____
_____
_____
_____
_____
_____
_____
_____
_____
_____
_____
_____
_____

DAY 60

BELIEVE IT OR NOT

It is truly about what we believe!

We really are astounding beings.

We can believe in a way no other creation can!

Why waste this gift by believing negativity into existence.

Focus on positivity, love, happiness, and prosperity and you will attract more of the like into your life.

What is a belief that has been limiting you? Is it true?

DAY 60

BELIEVE IT OR NOT

What is a belief that has been limiting you? Is it true?

THOUGHTS/ACTION STEPS

DAY 61
JUST BREATHE!

We see it all the time--elderly people talking about what they wish they had done earlier in life.

On your deathbed you rarely regret the things you did; you regret the things you were too afraid to do.

Let's promise ourselves to do everything we dream of.

We can then breathe our last breath knowing we did all we desired!

Take a breath.

DAY 61

JUST BREATHE!

THOUGHTS/ACTION STEPS

DAY 62
<u>WORK IT</u>

There is nothing like just going for it—
giving it your all.

Take a big bite out of life and work it
to the best of your ability.

Don't even give a second thought to
whether or not you can digest it!

After all, you never know unless you
try.

And chances are, you won't choke and
you won't die.

When was the last time you gave
something your all?

DAY 62

WORK IT

When was the last time you gave something your all?

THOUGHTS/ACTION STEPS

DAY 63

RIGHTFULLY YOURS

If you cannot visualize it, you will never achieve it!

Imagine yourself right on the brink of your dream.

Yes—that one! It's just right there waiting for you.

Destiny is within reach.

Eliminate any distractions and focus on it.

It is yours for the taking!

Create or add to your vision board today.

DAY 63

<u>RIGHTFULLY YOURS</u>

Create or add to your vision board today.

THOUGHTS/ACTION STEPS

_____

_____

_____

_____

_____

_____

_____

_____

_____

_____

_____

_____

_____

_____

DAY 64
SUCCESS SQUAD

Birds of a feather flock together.

If you mingle with them, you learn their ways.

I am sure you have heard these.

Well, here's another one: They are either supporting you or hurting you.

Take charge! Remain in a healthy, nurturing, positive, supportive environment.

Guard your goals and dreams as if your very existence depended upon them—because it does!

Are the 5 people you spend the majority of your time with supportive?

DAY 64

SUCCESS SQUAD

Are the 5 people you spend the majority of
your time with supportive?

THOUGHTS/ACTION STEPS

DAY 65
ASK AND RECEIVE

If you want it, just ask for it and expect to get it. I mean really prepare for its arrival.

See the floodgates open and good things pouring into your life.

You **CAN** have abundance in all areas: relationships, finances, and state of mind. You need only **ASK**.

What expectations will you set for the next 30 days?

DAY 65

ASK AND RECEIVE

What expectations will you set for the next 30 days?

THOUGHTS/ACTION STEPS

DAY 66

FALSE EVIDENCE APPEARING REAL

Fear is simply something we create in our heads of all the ways things could possibly go wrong.

We make up these horrible stories in our minds for one **BIG** reason; lack of faith in ourselves.

Faith trumps fear any day.

Focus on what can go right and truly believe in your inner power.

After all, fear is only false evidence.

DAY 66

FALSE EVIDENCE APPEARING REAL

THOUGHTS/ACTION STEPS

DAY 67
FLOOR IT!

If you're not willing to go for it how will you know what you could have accomplished?

Coulda, shoulda, woulda, is no alibi. Push it to the max—no regrets, no holds barred.

Put that pedal to the metal. Let the world see what you are made of.

Step out of that comfort zone and stay out. Make it a way of life.

Take some risks—reap some rewards.

What area of your life could use a little more gas?

DAY 67

FLOOR IT!

What area of your life could use a little more gas?

THOUGHTS/ACTION STEPS

DAY 68

PICK YOUR PAIN

Pain is something we will feel no matter what!

The question we must ask ourselves is this...which pain will hit the hardest and burn the longest?

Will it be the pain of discipline or regret? I guarantee it will be the pain of regret and disappointment.

That is a pain that will linger--maybe forever.

What areas could you use a little more discipline?

DAY 68
PICK YOUR PAIN

What areas could you use a little more discipline?

THOUGHTS/ACTION STEPS

DAY 69

HOW DEEP IS YOUR BELIEF

It has been said by many great souls who walked the earth: What we truly desire and believe we will get--we will attain.

We can have anything in this world we put our hearts and minds to, with faith.

Sometimes it appears the things we want don't come fast enough.

It is simply a matter of the depth of our belief.

Reconfirm your beliefs.

DAY 69

HOW DEEP IS YOUR BELIEF

Reconfirm your beliefs.

THOUGHTS/ACTION STEPS

DAY 70

STRUGGLE TO STRENGTH

Most of us have heard the saying "what doesn't kill me, makes me stronger." I would add, "if I learn and grow from it".

Getting beat up over and over again in life does not mean we were meant to live in pain.

The pain we endured in the past allows us to develop our strengths and know what sweet victory tastes like.

Recall an obstacle which allowed you to grow.

DAY 70

STRUGGLE TO STRENGTH

Recall an obstacle which allowed you to grow.

THOUGHTS/ACTION STEPS

DAY 71

<u>AMAZING ME</u>

We should work on creating an amazing relationship with ourselves.

People will come and go, some loyal some deceiving.

But we will have to live with ourselves for well...as long as we live.

Become someone that you can be proud of.

Follow your dreams, achieve your goals, and live everyday like it is especially yours.

How will you celebrate YOU today?

DAY 71

AMAZING ME

How will you celebrate YOU Today?

THOUGHTS/ACTION STEPS

DAY 72
WINNERS MAKE COMMITMENTS

Nobody likes to be left hanging!

Either you keep your commitments or you don't. There's no gray area.

Winners do not break promises (at least not without notification).

Form the habit of following through.

Commitment is one of the key ingredients to better relationships.

Make it a point to keep all your commitments for at least the next seven days.

DAY 72

WINNERS MAKE COMMITMENTS

Make it a point to keep all your commitments for at least the next seven days.

THOUGHTS/ACTION STEPS

DAY 73

THE GREAT DISCOVERY

We are where we are for a reason.

Our mission is to discover what that reason is; and we can start by exploring the opportunities all around us.

They exist—clues are everywhere, we need only be receptive.

Think of a time you missed out on an opportunity.

What did you learn?

DAY 73

THE GREAT DISCOVERY

Think of a time you missed out on an opportunity.

What did you learn?

THOUGHTS/ACTION STEPS

DAY 74
THE GROWTH CHALLENGE

Embrace challenging problems for in them lies your success.

In them lies the ability to not only overcome, but to realize your full potential. In them lies--your future.

Reflect back on a challenge and appreciate your growth.

DAY 74

THE GROWTH CHALLENGE

Reflect back on a challenge and appreciate your growth.

THOUGHTS/ACTION STEPS

DAY 75
<u>IT'S DINNER TIME</u>

You can wait for your fortune--but the secret is to **WORK** while you wait.

The saying is, "Good things come to those who wait".

The reality is, good things come to those who work.

Then, when you finally make it to the dining table of success, you will be able to partake in the feast of a lifetime.

DAY 75

IT'S DINNER TIME

THOUGHTS/ACTION STEPS

DAY 76

UNSTOPPABLE

You must have this commitment, you must have this drive, you must have this fortitude—let **NO ONE** or **NOTHING** stop you.

Ask no questions, create no excuses, accept no alibis.

Your vehicle for success must be fueled by passion!

What is your life purpose?

DAY 76

UNSTOPPABLE

What is your life purpose?

THOUGHTS/ACTION STEPS

DAY 77

YOUR BIGGEST ALLY

You will always be your biggest critic (although others may come pretty close).

But, you must also be your biggest ally.

No one should believe in you more than you believe in yourself.

Your thoughts are your strongest weapons don't use them against yourself.

Are you the captain of your team?

DAY 77

YOUR BIGGEST ALLY

Are you the captain of your team?

THOUGHTS/ACTION STEPS

_____

_____

_____

_____

_____

_____

_____

_____

_____

_____

_____

_____

_____

DAY 78

<u>THE WATER'S FINE</u>

Either you want to wade around all your life or you want to jump in and start swimming.

It's ok to start out in the kiddie pool, but your goal should be the ocean.

You can swim with sharks or play with the minnows, it is totally up to you.

Isn't it time to make some motion in the ocean?

DAY 78

THE WATER'S FINE

Isn't it time to make some motion in the ocean?

THOUGHTS/ACTION STEPS

DAY 79
UNCHAINED

Incarceration of the mind can be just as debilitating as being in a jail cell.

Why sentence yourself to a life of imprisonment. You have the key!

Create your own fate by breaking free of mental bondage.

Identify and release a mental block.

DAY 79

UNCHAINED

Identify and release a mental block.

THOUGHTS/ACTION STEPS

DAY 80

MIND FUEL

Books are simply made up of words
and words of letters.

Yet, it is the meditating on and
internalizing of these words that
invigorate the mind.

The brain craves intellectual
stimulation.

THINK about what
you just read.

DAY 80

MIND FUEL

THINK about what you just read.

THOUGHTS/ACTION STEPS

DAY 81

SET FREE

Make it real in your mind and it will become real in your life. Take mental inventory.

What you truly believe will show through your actions.

The truth will **SET YOU FREE.**

But it all begins--with your beliefs.

Actively monitor your thoughts throughout the day.

DAY 81

SET FREE

Actively monitor your thoughts throughout the day.

THOUGHTS/ACTION STEPS

DAY 82
OH, MY MISTAKE

Some say there are no mistakes, only opportunities for improvement.

Others say mistakes are simply the discovery of what doesn't work.

Any way you look at it, you have to be doing something to make them.

So do something—make the mistakes, discover the opportunities and repeat the process.

That's what success is all about.
Get used to it!

DAY 82
OH, MY MISTAKE
THOUGHTS/ACTION STEPS

DAY 83
YOUR MOMENT

Don't wait for someone else to change. It might not be their moment—it might not be their time.

Step to the plate! They can't see what you can—the vision is yours alone.

And, therefore the change must be made by YOU.

Who have you been waiting on and why?

DAY 83

YOUR MOMENT

Who have you been waiting on and why?

THOUGHTS/ACTION STEPS

DAY 84
AMAZING CONVICTION

Belief is defined as "something one accepts as true or real; a firmly held opinion or conviction."

So I ask you—what is that "something" that you have accepted? What are YOU holding fast to?

How convicted are you?

Go ahead AMAZE yourself, and others!

DAY 84

AMAZING CONVICTION

THOUGHTS/ACTION STEPS

DAY 85
<u>REST ASSURED</u>

You want to have a good day?

You want to rest well at night?

Then do something with the day! Don't sit around complaining about your circumstances.

Get out of the bed, get off the sofa, and **CHANGE** them. Be productive— learn, read, write, pursue, satisfaction starts and ends with **YOU**.

Set the intention for what you'd like to accomplish today.

DAY 85

REST ASSURED

Set the intention for what you'd like to accomplish today.

THOUGHTS/ACTION STEPS

DAY 86
THE GIVING GAME

We have all heard, "it is more blessed to give, than to receive". Give your attention.

Be genuinely interested not only in what others have to say; but in their lives.

Share in their joys, sorrows, and accomplishments. Listen with your heart.

Practice giving eye contact and giving your undivided attention.

DAY 86

THE GIVING GAME

Practice giving eye contact and giving
your undivided attention.

THOUGHTS/ACTION STEPS

DAY 87
TRAVEL BY BRAIN

Do you like where you are? Is it deserving of you?

Whether the answer be yes or no, you have only your thoughts to blame.

They can take you to the highest high or the lowest low.

THINK about where you would like to go!

Whatever thoughts came to mind put them to paper.

DAY 87

TRAVEL BY BRAIN

Whatever thoughts came to mind put them to paper.

THOUGHTS/ACTION STEPS

DAY 88
<u>NEWS WORTHY</u>

There certainly is enough negativity to read and listen to.

We are inundated with sad news stories from around the world.

Why not balance it out, at least a little, with something positive, something that will actually help rather than hinder.

Not only will your day start and end on a much better note; but the time in between will be more productive and enjoyable as well.

Think on these things!

DAY 88

<u>NEWS WORTHY</u>

Think on these things!

THOUGHTS/ACTION STEPS

DAY 89
WHAT'S YOUR FLAVOR?

You don't have to recreate the wheel!!

Take an idea that you believe to have potential and mold it into what you have envisioned... you-style.

Don't worry about your creation being similar to something people have heard or seen before because

YOU have never done it before.

Give it your flavor!

Revisit an old idea with a new perspective.

DAY 89

WHAT'S YOUR FLAVOR?

Revisit an old idea with a new perspective.

THOUGHTS/ACTION STEPS

DAY 90
ROCKY ROAD

Life becomes easier as a result of the obstacles we overcome.

Don't always look for the path of least resistance.

Strength is often found on the rocky road.

As the saying goes, what doesn't kill you; makes you stronger--though it may be difficult and take a little longer.

How has an obstacle you have overcome, improved your quality of life today?

DAY 90

ROCKY ROAD

How has an obstacle you have overcome, improved your quality of life today?

THOUGHTS/ACTION STEPS

DAY 91

<u>SOUL SURVIVOR</u>

You can gain any material pleasure
your heart desires, but don't lose sight
of your standards and values.

Treat yourself and others with
care and love.

Never forget who you are or let worldly
possessions change you for the worse.

If you lose your soul you
are worth-less.

DAY 91

SOUL SURVIVOR

THOUGHTS/ACTION STEPS

DAY 92

WHERE IS THE LOVE?

Remove the obstacles, the blockages and you will realize that love is there.

Let it flow freely through every aspect of your life.

Simply invite it into your body, your home, your work place, and your state of mind.

Where and how could you spread more love?

DAY 92

WHERE IS THE LOVE?

Where and how could you spread more love?

THOUGHTS/ACTION STEPS

DAY 93
GOAL MIND

Striking out on a journey without a map wastes a lot of time and energy.

No matter how intelligent we may be, we all need a little guidance! Detours and delays come in all forms and are inevitable.

But, we must keep our goals foremost in our minds. For not only do goals build courage and wisdom--they change lives.

What life-changing goal have you been afraid to set? Set it!

DAY 93
GOAL MIND

What life-changing goal have you been afraid to set? Set it!

THOUGHTS/ACTION STEPS

_____

_____

_____

_____

_____

_____

_____

_____

_____

_____

_____

_____

_____

_____

_____

DAY 94
<u>DOCTOR'S ORDERS</u>

Laughter truly is the best medicine, at any age!

And unless we can continue to laugh in the midst of disappointments, setbacks, and trials, life will hold little joy for us.

Nobody likes a grouchy old man—or a grouchy **YOUNG** woman, for that matter.

We should laugh at 90 like we did at 9.

Why take life so seriously?

The older we get, the more there is to laugh about.

So look life square in the face—and **LAUGH!**

DAY 94

DOCTOR'S ORDERS

THOUGHTS/ACTION STEPS

DAY 95

<u>DO IT NOW</u>

When you feel it, reveal it!

Don't trust yourself to remember the next day or the next hour even.

Get up and start writing, drawing, speaking, whatever it is.

Because once it's gone, it may never return again in exactly the same way.

Strike while the iron is HOT!!

Have easy access to a journal or tablet for these times.

DAY 95

DO IT NOW

THOUGHTS/ACTION STEPS

DAY 96

OVERFLOW

You must give to get.

Step out on faith and put it to the test!

Then stand back and watch the overflow. Just watch how much more you receive.

Not only will windows open, but doors as well.

And you will simply have to share.

How can you start the sharing process today?

DAY 96
OVERFLOW
How can you start the sharing process today?
THOUGHTS/ACTION STEPS

DAY 97
PURSUIT OF HAPPINESS

Be happy as you journey toward your mission.

Enjoy the quest as it unfolds.

Take each step with energy and enthusiasm knowing you are that much closer to your dream.

With this mental state, happiness and fulfillment will most assuredly find you!

Make yourself a happy list and read aloud.

DAY 97
PURSUIT OF
HAPPINESS

Make yourself a happy list and read aloud.

THOUGHTS/ACTION STEPS

DAY 98

OUT-STANDING

Fit in---to what?

Why would you want to be another carbon copy?

Create your own life!

You be the benchmark—you set the standard, you make the difference!

Stand up, speak out and break the mold.

Do something big, do something--
BOLD!!!

When is the last time you

STOOD--OUT?

DAY 98

OUT-STANDING

When is the last time you STOOD--OUT?

THOUGHTS/ACTION STEPS

DAY 99

YOUR ERRAND

Now you have been enlightened.

How are you fulfilling your mission?

It could be as simple as sharing a smile or as complex as discovering the next medical cure.

Whether large or small, you have an obligation to answer the call.

Will you rise to the occasion?

DAY 99

<u>YOUR ERRAND</u>

Will you rise to the occasion?

THOUGHTS/ACTION STEPS

DAY 100

BONUS DAY

Why a bonus day? Always give a little extra, plain and simple. And what better day to write your 100-year plan than DAY 100? Yes that's correct, 100 YEAR PLAN!

Does the name Napoleon Hill ring a bell? He was born in 1883. He died almost 50 years ago. We are still thinking and growing rich--today! (Read the book.)

The butterfly does not exist very long, but it is beautiful while it's here. We, on the other hand have the unique fortune to extend our beauty for an eternity.

Life is about generating a light so bright, it is still shining 50--75--100 years from now.

Are you with us?

Let's illuminate the world, COLLECTIVELY.

Here's to 100 years!

CONTACT THE AUTHORS

Speaking inquiries & Workshops:
info@thinkonthesethingsbook.com

QuentinMcCain.com

Book info & other:
ThinkonTheseThingsBook.com

Thank you for your purchase.

This book has been an amazing project for us!

We truly hope you enjoyed reading this book as much as we did writing it.

Sincerely,

**Quentin McCain
&
E. Marie Hall**

Made in the USA
San Bernardino, CA
26 July 2016